Daniil Dragos

Was an engineer in oil rigs manufacturing in Ploiesti. He worked for Control Data Corporation - USA, in Research and Development and later on as Market Development Manager for East Europe (computer sales and the first postwar American manufacturing joint venture in Eastern Europe). He worked in Research and Development in Automation and computers in Bucharest. Was a counselor and Deputy Director in the Ministry of Foreign Trade - Bucharest (negotiations of Cernavoda Nuclear Power Plant, of cars manufacturing with Renault and Citroen - France etc.). He was a Fulbright Visiting Scholar at Graduate School of Management, University of California, Los Angeles (UCLA). He is an author of books and articles.

Daniil Dragos

O Domine, Quo Vadis our world?!

ISBN: 9781688915572

DEDICATION

I dedicate this essay to the people who acknowledge the transient nature of all earthly goods and pursuits.

CONTENTS

My first discussion with a cultivated and friendly American   7-24

My next discussion with the same cultivated and friendly American   25-69

Motto:
'There are more things in heaven and earth, Horatio, than are dreamt of in your philosophy."
William Shakespeare, (1564 - 1616);
"We can know only that we know nothing. And that is the highest degree of human wisdom."
Leo Tolstoy (1828 - 1910).

1)- *My first discussion with a cultivated and friendly American*

From time to time, actually I discussed with my American friends, about some important topics of our world, i.e. war, environmental degradation, inequality between people and countries, migrants and globalization. Looking around and seeing what happens nowadays, we were asking ourselves: O Domine, Quo Vadis our world?!. Maybe it is unusual the fact that those serious subjects were discussed by some Americans -the citizens of the only superpower today- and myself, a citizen of a country considered to be, in the European Union, one of the two most corrupt and poor countries. As far as I remember, the opinions expressed are those represented below. I have to admit that some exposed opinions could be subjective and wrong. However, we endeavored to tell the truth and nothing but the truth. The whole truth could not be told; that is known only to God Almighty. Anyway, let me present the said discussions; in other words, let start working, as the peasants used to say in the Transylvanian village where I was born.

In May-June of the year 1999, I was in the United States. While NATO bombing in Yugoslavia was taking place in force, I was invited to a party by Bill Rogers, an acquaintance of Susan, my American daughter-in-law. If during the time I was an employee of an American multinational computer manufacturing corporation called CDC (1970-75), I was amazed that Americans had near to a hundred dissimilar opinions about the Vietnam War, every one being most critical, this time there was only one conviction, namely that Milosevic and the Serbs were bloody torturers, and Albanians -especially those in Kosovo- were all innocent martyrs. This opinion, summary in fact, was presented also briefly but daily on the TV. I had the feeling that if someone had the audacity to support another view, no matter how different, it would have borne the abuse of the American public.

Bill's house was located on the edge of one of the lakes called Finger Lakes. The party took place in the shadow of towering and shady trees on a lawn that stretched between the house and the lake. Looking the guests' cars, the appetizing sirloin beef steaks on the grill, the abundant drinks of all kinds, you could see that we were socializing with middle-class Americans. After a short swimming in the cold water of the lake, I was invited by Bill for a short fishing trip. Despite the modern fishing gear and the fact that the boat was equipped with sonar to detect the fish, the damn fish were not impressed, so we caught no fish. Then Bill invited me to his office. Suddenly, he approached precisely the subject of which, that time, I was avoiding in my discussions with Americans.

- "What do you think of the war against Yugoslavia?"

- "As my only son Daniel works in the United States and hopes to become a citizen of this country, my views coincide with those I see almost all the Americans have. I also want to tell you that my grandfather, the father of my father, lived in America for 24 years and was an American citizen. So what can I tell you? The US punishes the wicked and defends the weak and the poor. In other words, the good cowboys fight, against the bad guys!" That's how I avoided Bill's question.

- "Well, well... But if your son would not work in the United States, and if your grandfather had not been an American citizen, what would you think? I think we can have a sincere discussion, like civilized people... It's a free country after all!"

Intimately I was on high alert. Shall I engage in such a discussion? I only knew Bill for a very short time. He looked like a good man. But I do know that all over the world, sincerity only brings you inconveniences. I decided to be cautious, but not to tell lies.

- "OK, Bill. For the beginning, let's forget my personal opinions, or more precisely, as you Americans are saying forget my feelings, let's just keep in mind that I am a European, plus I have to tell you that history is my hobby. So, I do know that at the beginning of the eighth century, Muslim Arabs entered the Southwest of Europe, managing to occupy almost the entire territory of Spain. The complete end of the Arab occupation in Spain takes place only in 1492, the year when Columbus discovered America. In 11th and 12th centuries, the Muslim Turks entered the South East of Europe. Until 1453, when Constantinople fell, the Turks were able to occupy the entire Byzantine Empire. The Turkish Muslims have reached the gates of Vienna two times; last time in 1683. The Romanians, Orthodox Christians, have been centuries under the suzerainty of Turkish-Ottoman Muslims. Many of today's troubles of the Romanians are due to these centuries of Turkish seizure. The misery with which we Romanians are struggling; moral damages too... The Turkish Muslims have been a real curse on the heads of Romanians and of other peoples of Southeast Europe. If the Romanians, the Greeks, the Serbs, the Slovenians, the Bulgarians, the Albanians and the Croats had been subjected (for four centuries!) to more enlightened nations, such as the English, Germans, or French, another would have been the situation in this part of Europe today; and maybe worldwide too. It was only in 1877, a century after you Americans liberated yourselves, that we managed finally to escape from the wild and cruel Turks, and Romania became independent.

- "What does all this have to do with my question regarding our planes bombing Yugoslavia?"

- "I think that's a sensible question, Bill, because I have come to the conclusion that we are witnessing, without realizing, a new Muslim expansion in Europe, and not just in Europe! This time, there is not an expansion by fire and sword as it was in the past. It is mostly an expansion caused by a demographic explosion and the huge gap between rich and poor countries. I do not know if you did read the writings of an American called Samuel Huntington? The views that I have come to at present time are based, to a large extent, on the judgments of his book titled *The Clash of Civilizations'*. I've read some statistics regarding the situation after the First World War. That time, Romania had a population of about 16 million, and Turkey about 14 million. Today, my country has 22 million inhabitants, and Turkey over 60 million. Romania's population is continuously decreasing, while in Muslim Turkey is growing steadily. In the former Yugoslavia, the share of Muslim populations has increased enormously. In Kosovo, the Muslim population became predominant, though it was once a minority. Let us admit that the good people, i. e. the Bosnian and Albanian Muslims, must be supported in their struggle against the wicked Serbian Christians. But in that case how do we stay regarding the Muslims expansion in Europe? Even in Romania the Muslim population - Arabians and Turks - grows year after year. In our country there is also an economic expansion; they already own part of the country's land, industry and trade. Most vegetables are imported from Turkey by the Turks. In Germany live millions of Muslims. If Christians Fritz or Hans had gone to Islam, it would have been altogether different! Unfortunately, the Muslims are Turks brought to work, or their children born in Germany and becoming German citizens. They say that Berlin has the largest Turkish population after Istanbul! In France, the Muslims are not made up of French Catholics converted to Islam, but of Algerians and other foreigners who have come to a better life in that country. A similar phenomenon of Muslims infusion also occurs in the UK, and even in the United States. For various reasons, including religious ones, the birthrate of the Muslims is much higher than that of European Christians or native European nations, that is, those called 'Caucasians' by you Americans. In fact, the birthrate of all nations in Africa, Asia, the Middle East and Latin America is much higher. Mainly, due the huge gap between rich and poor countries, the peoples from that part of the world started to move toward the rich countries of the West. The local wars, represent only the second most important reason of this phenomenon. If the current pace of arrivals from Africa, Asia, the Middle East, Latin America, etc.

continues, the demographic structure will change radically in the rich countries of the West. By the way, I just remember the old *'Drang nach Osten'* of the Germans. I read on the Internet that on February 7, 1945, when it was quite clear that Germany had lost the war, Hitler said: *'It is eastwards, only and always eastwards, that is the veins of our race must expand, that.is the direction in which the expansion of our German race must take place. It is the direction Nature intended for the expanses of the German people.'* Strange enough, nowadays *de facto*, it is mainly *Drang nach* Germany and generally *nach* to the whole West. So, in that part of the world the demographic structure will change drastically; i. e. the percentage of what you Americans call Caucasians will diminish."

- "We say that in the United States it is different. Here there is a sort of *melting pot* in which all religions, races, and ethnic groups mingle with each other, merge and eventually reach a single entity. We have seen your Europeans considerations, let's say that they are one hundred percent correct. And suppose that are true all they say about the Kosovar Albanian Muslims. In that case is it good or bad, that we are bombarding Yugoslavia?!"

- "In my capacity as an European, and in view of everything I have told you, I do not know how I could answer your question. But Bill, after my long speech, as you said, I would like to hear your opinion. That would be fair!"

- "You started on the easiest way. But I must admit that it is still fair. My views are confusing, or rather, not yet definitive. A few days ago I talked to a friend, a young pilot who had just returned from a Yugoslav bombing raid. At my insistence, he told me about those bombings. I must tell you that I am also a hunter. When the pilot were telling me, how he was looking to the radar screen and pushed the button to launch the rocket against a tank, bridge, refinery, or building, I had the impression that we were listening to our hunting stories, which usually we were telling after shooting a wolf, a bear or a deer. Everything was said calmly, and he seemed satisfied with what he had done. When I asked him if he was concerned that in the targets were human beings, he answered me plainly, *'they all of them are just real bastards'*. That statement made me think. Today we believe what we are told, that all Serbs are wicked and bastards. But if, in a few years' time, it will happen as was the case of Japanese attack of Pearl Harbor on December 7, 1941, or the assassination of J. F. Kennedy?! Then also, we believed everything the Establishment told us! But later on, we learned that the Japanese attack of Pearl Harbor was known before, but no action was taken so as to determine US's entry into the Second World War. As for Kennedy's assassination, other variants than the official one were circulated. If tomorrow, it turns out, that there were villains between Albanian Muslims in Kosovo too, then how will we be able to revive the innocent among the Serbs who are now considered the only bastards? On the other hand, in my heart, I feel proud that my country is the only super power in the world, and as such, it seeks to maintain a fair order across the planet."

- "Being the citizens of the only superpower in the world, are you Americans happier than the Swiss, let say? They have about the same standard of living and civilization as you the Americans, though they are the citizens of a small country. Are they less happy for this reason? "

- "I do not know. But as far as I'm concerned, being an American makes me feel good anywhere I am, in New York, Tokyo, Beijing, Paris, or in the heart of Africa in Kinshasa let say."

- "That reminds me of an experiment I made at home in Bucharest. I was just reading a book titled *'From the Psychology of the Romanian People'* (by Draghicescu). It describes the national characteristics of different nations. I read to my wife the characteristics of the Germans, the Russians, the French and the Italians, telling her every time what nationality they were referring to. Then I read some characteristics without telling her to whom they were referring to. I asked her to tell me what nation it was about. She immediately replied that they were certainly the national characteristics of the Americans. Just find out that the answer was wrong. I read the characteristics of the Romans during the Roman Empire's maximum power. At that time, they were convinced that they were dominating the whole world, not knowing probably that at the other end of the earth there was another great empire called China. Interestingly, the Romans, the masters of the *'world'* that time, had exactly the psychology the Americans have today. It was specified, including the fact that they felt safe *'all over the world'*. It can be inferred that in two thousand years man has progressed from a technological point of view, in organization and management, but psychologically and morally remained the same. The man, the king of the animals, remained with the same instincts and tendencies; his human nature has not changed."

- "I do not know what the ancient Romans would think about the bombing of the bridges in Yugoslavia by the Americans, including those across the Danube. The bridge built by Apolodor from Damascus, for Emperor Trajan to pass his legions to your ancient Dacia, had escaped; that one had escaped the bombardment because it was demolished many centuries before. But why do you seem amazed? Do you think only you know history?! Find out that my profession leaves me enough time to read. I am an accounting expert and I work on my own. I do expertise and accounting reviews for small businesses, but also for some larger companies. My earnings are directly linked to the course of the American economy. So, by the number of dollars that enter in my pocket, I can feel its pulse. Since the bombings in Yugoslavia, my proceeds have increased. I'm also investing in the Stock Exchange. And there I gain better and better. The better the course of military industry goes, we Americans are more prosperous. Not only the American economy goes better; all the world economy is progressing! The aftermath of the big crisis, which began at Wall Street in 1929, was wiped out by the World War II arms building. So it could be concluded that the wars are useful too. But than what about the teachings of the New Testament?"

- "What can I say?! Just that's a good question! But let me introduce another aspect to you. Since 1970, when I came to work for an American corporation, I used to wear pajamas and underwear made in America by *'Fruit of the Loom'*. They were cheap and of good quality. Last week I walked through countless shops to buy pajamas and underwear *'Made in USA'*. I did not find anywhere. Since the *'globalization'*, most of US consumer goods are being made in countries like

China, Mexico, Taiwan, Nicaragua, India, etc. Most probably only high-tech products will be manufactured in the United States."

- "I do not think that only high technology productions, along with the military industries, can ensure the long-term prosperity of the American citizens. Then we have to acknowledge that eventually the production of too many weapons leads to their use. So, let us ask ourselves if we, who praise us that we are Christians, respect or not the precepts of Jesus Christ."

Here I interrupted him again, telling him about Kiki Péter, a nice but crazy old man from the village where I was born. Based on his participation in the World War I battles and the passage of the Second World War front over our village, he concluded that the war would become more and more expensive. Eliminating enemy soldiers and taking prisoners, he said, cost and will cost more and more with the passage of time. He claimed that in the end, only the US will have enough money to carry important and long wars.

- "Dan, you have to admit that the old Kiki Péter was not that crazy! Of course, his claims are sinister, but the war is sinister, even though it was practiced and will be practiced by people thought to be rational and serious. The Old Man said that the effectiveness of the war is determined by the ratio of spending against the number of enemy soldiers destroyed or taken prisoners, and that with the passage of the years this ratio is getting higher, which means that the effectiveness of the war is always decreasing. He was right! Look the bombing in Yugoslavia. Enormous spending and damages! However, only about 1,000 people died. Probably not half of them were military. In Vietnam and Cambodia, more bombs and artillery shells were fired than in the Second World War; all that with huge expenses and damages. From the media it results that about 3 million Indo-Chinese and 50,000 Americans died. That is, human losses were much lower than the tens of millions of deaths of the Second World War. The most *'efficient'* killing power per unit of time had the two atomic bombs thrown by President Truman over Hiroshima and Nagasaki. There, however, few soldiers died, the vast majority being civilians. The nuclear weapons have been developed and are manufactured with astronomical costs. About the effectiveness of these weapons what can we say?! If one side would use them massively, and the other side would retaliate, their *'efficiency'* as a power of destruction would make life disappear on our planet."

- "Kiki Péter did not know anything about nuclear bombs." I intervened. "He was referring to the classic war... "

- "There were a lot of others who had thought about the connection between war and money. I was reading somewhere that a king or emperor in Europe -there were too many of them, so I forgot which one of them- had to give up the war that was planned, because Rothschild refused to lend him money. For war, you need money, money and money again! The Old Man may also be right when he claims that in the future only the United States will have enough money to carry wars, especially the extensive ones. It seems that you have not noticed that in the Persian Gulf War and in the war in Yugoslavia, the participation of our European allies were symbolic. We must not forget, however, that the Old Man formed his theories on the basis of his experience in the First World War and of what he had seen in 1944 on the occasion of crossing the front line through your village in Transylvania. But let's see how an US military expert will think. Let's put ourselves in his shoes! He will say that the war must be won, with minimal material expenses and, if possible, zero personal losses. In theory, that means efficiency for him. Ours will strive to protect the lives of the American military men to the maximum. If too many of our boys are killed, American public opinion will get angry, and there may be a repetition of what happened during the Vietnam War. Those at the top of the power pyramid (the *'Establishment'*) would not like that. At material expenses, it is quite different. Let's imagine that we would win a war in a few days, and after we've lost only two helicopters, one F-16 and we've only launched 10 cruise missiles. Such a war is not worth starting! What profits can such a war bring?!

How long it will give work to our arms factories? You will argue that armaments wear out morally in time, which is why they should be replaced periodically even in peacetime. It's true... But one is the demand for weaponry in peacetime, and another is demand in wartime. Didn't you say that consumer goods are no longer produced in America?! Well, did you see?! If the demand for military equipment catastrophically decreases, what we Americans will still produce?"

- "If the *'Establishment'* or those who decide the fate of the world think so, it means that Peace has no chance. No chance, at all! ..."

- "Could you, Dan, prove to me that, with the passage of time, there were less and less wars? If there were wars in the past, why would not they exist in the future as well? You just did say that from the time of the ancient Romans to this day, the human nature did not change."

- "Everything you said, Bill, makes me think. You also mentioned that in order to put an end to the American *'isolationism'* that existed after the First World War, were not been taken any actions, even though it was known before that the Japanese will attack Pearl Harbor... "

- "In the American public opinion of that time, was heavily rooted the idea that we no longer had to mingle ourselves in the mess of a new European war. And as I explained it to you, the *'Establishment'* had to take public opinion into account."

- "I understand Bill... It seems to me that you think that not all countries are equal."

-"Dan, Dan... *O, my goodness,* the countries have not been, nor will they ever be equal." Our declaration of independence states that all men are created equal, so men are created equal, but later on even they, I mean the Americans, are no longer equal. The countries have not even been created equal!"

- "All men are created equal! Maybe in the sense that, finally, all die. The rich and all powerful of the world, die like the poor, humiliated pauper. We have given our opinion about the war, in general, and about the Second World War in particular. Have you not noticed that the main characters on which the evolutions of the Second World War depended suddenly died?! F. D. Roosevelt died at the age of 63 on April 12, 1945; before the surrender of Germany. Hitler committed suicide on April 30, 1945, eight days after his 56th birthday. Thus, after only 12 years, the *'Deutches Reich of a thousand years'* ended. Stalin lived less than eight years after the end of World War II."

- "You might be right, Dan. I know what you mean. In support of what you said is the fact that the great conquerors of the world have died unexpectedly and quite young. After conquering a good part of the world, Alexander Macedon died at the age of 32. Another great military genius, Julius Caesar, was stabbed by several plotters in the *Capitol* of Rome. He was less than 56 when he died.

Napoleon died in exile on a isolated island at a relatively young age of 52. Some say he was poisoned."

- "That's right, Bill... Lenin, the creator of the Soviet empire, died when he was less than 54 years old. This was probably also due to the fact that on August 30, 1918, he was shot by Fania Kaplan, a member of the Revolutionary Socialist Party. Lenin was neither general nor a great conqueror, but more a *'library mouse'*. But if he had not been born, the Russian empire would have broken down after the First World War. The results would have been the same as when Gorbachev and Yeltsin later on actually disintegrated the USSR. Due to Lenin, the Russian Empire survived another 73 years. I have examples from my country's recent history as well. Marshal Antonescu, who had been the dictator of Romania during the Second World War, was tried and shot in 1946, when he was not yet 64 years old. The first communist dictator, Cheorghiu Dej, died in 1965, when he was less than 64 years old. Later, it was rumored that, as a result of his tendency to liquidate Romania's dependence on the USSR, he had been radiated by the Soviets. On the Christmas Day of 1989, following a one-hour and 20-minute trial masquerade, Dictator Ceausescu and his wife were shot."

- "Makes sense what you say, Dan... And yet all this does not teach the current or the future leaders to be less arrogant and undeserving. They have the impression that they are immortal, or that they will live for at least a thousand years. History did not teach the all powerful people of the world anything at all, nor will ever teach them!"

The discussion lasted a long time. Especially, as it was accompanied by plenty of whiskey. Bill had an extraordinary knowledge of culture and history. I was accustomed to look down on the Americans from the point of view of their culture. One of my friends in the US told me that this was the consequence of my inferiority complex toward the Americans. But Bill is more cultured and read more than me. I have to say that his name is not Bill Roger. Instead of saying, like newspapermen, that the interlocutor preferred to remain anonymous, I simply changed his name. Otherwise, if the American public at that time, and especially his clients, had been aware of his unconventional assertions, I am pretty sure that he would have lost at least 80% of the customers in his business as an accounting expert. This is a personal opinion, which may still be subjective. Bill did not ask me for our discussion to be off record. It's my decision, just to be on the safe side, as the Americans say.

2)- My next discussion with the same cultivated and friendly American

In February 2019, I received an email from Bill Rogers, suggesting that we should have a new discussion. He mentioned that if I was not about to take a trip to US, we could discuss on Skype.

I was really surprised, as I did not see Bill and did not hear anything from him since our discussion that took place at his house, in the period of May-June 1999. I asked myself, how the bloody hell he got my email address?! Thinking and thinking, in the end I came to the conclusion that he got my email address from Susan, my former American daughter-in-law. That was the truth. I have to point out that after nine years of marriage, my son Daniel and Susan divorced. Nevertheless, my wife and I did not interrupt our relation with Susan. By the way, I was quite pleased that she read the book that I published with a friend of mine and titled **'Europe: to be, or not to be - that is the Question!'** In January 20, 2018, she even sent me the following email: '*I am not a very political person, nor am I a historian. Therefore, I will leave that to Mr. Portzan, lest I be chastised! In my humble opinion, I believe that the state of political affairs has been, and continues to be, grounded in money, power and control. I know of no poor or middle class persons in congress, senate, presidency, etc. Money is power. Hence* *corporate greed; it's never enough. The divide widens. I believe the description of 'white supremacy' is accurate, although I would also add 'male' to that description. Patriarchy has been and remains strong. We continue to lobby for equality, not only for women, but for all. Hope you are both well. Congratulation for the book titled* **Europe: to be, or not to be - that is the Question!**, *Daniil, and for continuing to keep the conversation going. Susan.'* I have to point out that Susan is a bright person and she works as *a* probation officer in a county of New York State.

Surely, I agreed with Bill's suggestion, being quite willing to have a new discussion with such a cultivated and friendly person. So, several days after receiving the email sent by him, we had a new discussion. To decide the hour of our discussion on Skype, we had to take into consideration the fact that between his local US time and the Romanian local time there is a time gap of seven hours.- "Hi my friend!" I heard Bill's friendly voice.

- "It is nice talking to you! Long time passed, since we had that interesting discussion in May or June of the year 1999. Very nearly 20 years."

- "That's right and there were a lot of happenings since that time." Bill said.

- "Yes, I remember them all; like seeing them yesterday. I mean the September 11 attacks of 2001. They have been amazing and unexpected events for the whole world. Live on TV, we could all of us see a passenger plane hitting one of the two New

York skyscrapers called the World Trade Center Twin Towers. From the other tower there was already a thick smoke coming out of it, a sign that it has been hit before. After a while, I saw how the two towers collapsed one after the other. You felt like watching a science fiction movie. Everything seemed unreal! It was not an hour before, and on TV it was seen that flames and smoke were coming out from one of the five sides of the 'Pentagon' in Washington. The Pentagon Building had been also hit by a liner plane. Following the attacks, more than 3,000 people died. There have been direct and indirect material damages of many billions of dollars. The New York Stock Exchange was closed for several days. After its reopening, there was a sharp fall in stock prices. The US economy has entered into recession. As expected, the world economy did the same. Officially, it was reported that a New York and Washington attack had triggered a terrorist war of aggression against the United States (the only superpower on the planet now). As a result, the leaders of United States called for the establishment of a world coalition that would wage a relentless war against the international terrorism."

- "I saw those events many times on the TV. I guess that your description is quite accurate. On October 7, 2001, the United States and the United

Kingdom attacked Afghanistan with airplanes and cruise missiles. The Taliban fundamentalist Muslim movement, which was in power in that country, had not accepted to hand over Osama bin Laden and his accomplices, presumed guilty for the terrorist attacks in New York and Washington. Bin Laden was the head of Al-Qaeda Islamist fundamentalist terrorist network. At the same time, the media announced that isolated cases of biological attacks with anthrax bacilli have occurred in the United States. Subsequently, anthrax-contaminated letters were also detected in other countries. Day-by-day, the media announce new air strikes in Afghanistan and new sporadic cases of anthrax or false alarms with those bacilli. In Afghanistan, a small number of special commando land forces were also sent."

- "I asked myself, what's next? I did not know! But we did find out that many of the concepts of wars were radically changing. Not by accident, the most powerful leaders of the world have said that after September 11, 2001, the world will be different. So, it is assumed that all that American officials have said about the events correspond exactly to reality and truth. But Bill, you said that after a few years another truth might appear."

- "That's right. But for now, let's look at some of

the findings we can draw from the *'truth'* that is being preached to us today. Item **a)**. Napoleon, though he had been a great military genius, failed to cross the English Channel and carry the war on English soil. By bombing England with aviation and V1 and V2 missiles, Hitler managed to take this step. But no matter how many efforts he made to develop submarines and V2 missiles, he failed to break through the Atlantic Ocean and reach US territory. Japan had not been able to do that by breaking through the Pacific Ocean either. Bin Laden and his terrorists went further and hit targets in America's political and economic capital; Washington and New York respectively. And not any objectives, but the symbol of the military power represented by the Pentagon building, and the symbols of the American and world finances represented by the two Twin Towers. Thus, one after the other, the intangibility of the Great Britain, and then that of US provided by the Atlantic and Pacific Oceans, disappeared. Item **b)**. I read in a newspaper that Al-Qaeda spent about $ 500 million to organize and carry out the terrorist attacks of September 11, 2001. The loss of human lives and the direct and indirect damage resulting from these attacks were incomparably greater than those caused by spending the same amount of money in any of the twentieth century wars. Item **c)**. From the events of September 11, 2001 can be deduced that a terrorist organization, such as Al-Qaeda, can fight war against the most powerful and best-armed countries on the planet, though in terms of resources, funds and military technologies available to the two parts, there is a huge imbalance. So in the future could be big wars with less money. Item **d)**. If, as they say, the world is going to be different in the future, and the wars will go especially against terrorism, it means that the modern sophisticated weapons and their massive production will no longer have the same importance as before. Among other things, economic downturns will no longer be avoided by speeding up military productions. In anti-terrorist wars will not be possible to use atomic bombs, even less hydrogen bombs. Will there be a general nuclear disarmament? Nobody knows!"

- "I am not an expert in this field. I am a plain commoner. I would like to hear your opinion on the cold war. Mostly I am puzzled by the consequences of the cold war in both our countries. I read a lot about it; even books and much on the net too. I lived the whole cold war; from the start in 1947 till its end in 1991. Actually, in both our countries, the cold war had harsh consequences."

- "For an American, it is strange to hear such a statement!"

- "Maybe… But, do you think that now the common Americans live a better life than during the cold war of the seventies, for example? I was told by some of my American friends that nowadays, for the same standard of living, in an American family both husband and his wife have to get jobs; not just one of them as been the case in the seventies."

- "Still, it is not easy to accept that statement."

- "Then I will give you a few excerpts from President Trump Inauguration Address. *'Mothers and children trapped in poverty in our inner cities; rusted-out factories scattered like tombstones across the landscape of our nation... We've made other countries rich while the wealth, strength, and confidence of our country have disappeared over the horizon. One by one, the factories shuttered and left our shores, with not even a thought about the millions upon millions of American workers left behind.'* I think that all that President Trump said in his Inauguration Address is the truth and nothing but the truth."

- "Why do you think that the cold war have harsh consequences for Romania too?"

- "First of all, I will give you some excerpts from the book titled **'Europe: to be, or not to be - that is the Question!'** and read and commented by Susan. *'In 1989, the industrial infrastructure available to Romania has ranked her in the top 10 countries in Europe. This was largely based on technologies, know-how and manufacturing licenses imported from world-renowned companies, in US, Germany, France, England, Canada, Sweden, Japan, and so on. The greatest part of the above mentioned industrial infrastructure was built, during a short historical period, i.e. in 45 years of communist dictatorship. That* *was done through harsh sacrifice of the Romanians standard of living... Very little (less than 25%) of the industrial infrastructure existing in Romania in 1989 still has reality today; most of it was 'liquidated'. ... There was an extended deindustrialisation.'* I will add that close to 100% of the retail (hiprmarkets etc) is now in foreign ownership. Amost all the banks existing today in Romania are subsidiaries of banks located abroad; over 90% of the existing banking capital is foreign owned. Practically all the insuarance existing in Romania is owned by foreign companies. The Romanian comercial fleet (used to be the seventh in the world) and ocean fishing fleet (the second in Atlantic Ocean, after the soviet fleet) disappeared. By the way, after two world wars, Romania kept its control over its oil resources. Due to our wise politicians, for merely 668 million of euro, that control was lost after the end of the cold war. The *'de jure'* control over Romania's oil resources was won by an Austrian company (OMV). In a public speech, a former Romanian diplomat in Berlin stated that *'de facto'* control over the said oil resources was won by Germany. As, both on the western front and eastern front, Hitler had the power to dispose only on the Romanian oil resources, it would not have been politicaly correct to conclude openly that deal with a German company. The wages in Romania are between 5 and 9 times lower than those in Western European countries. As a result of all that, about half of Romania's employees (about 5 million, nobody knows the exact figure) emigrated. Today, more Romanians children are born abroad than inside Romania. Syria is the only country in the world from which more people emigrated than those that emigrated from Romania; but the Syrian emigration was caused by a long and cruel war. I am sorry for my too long explanation... Maybe, the reason is that the consequences are endured by me personally too."

- "I understand... I read quite a lot about Romania's position during cold war. I do know that two former *'communist'* countries, Yugoslavia and Romania, directly or indirectly, had supported the West and United States especially, in some of the most difficult phases of the long Cold War. The role of Romania is now well known and results from the publication, on the Internet, of transcripts of the conversations of Ceausescu with Henry Kissinger and President Nixon in US and Romania. The most amazing is the toast President Nixon's pronounced during Ceausescu's visit in USA in December 4-7, 1973. Paradoxically, after the collapse of the eastern bloc, Yugoslavia and Romania were most severely punished. Yugoslavia was dismantled and some of it bombed. Romania escaped with less harm; only its economy was destroyed! But, we spent too much on the topic, so that is enough... Let see how much were the US and USSR military expenditures. I read that the US military expenditures in the cold war had been estimated at $8 trillion. The financial cost for the Soviet Union was far higher than that of the United States. In any war, the winning side gets the gain. So, can you tell me which countries are the winners and which are the losers of the cold war?"

- "Bill, that's a sensible question! The official or *'de jure'* great winner of the cold war was your country, i.e. the United States of America. The great loser country was USSR. Strange enough is the fact that it seems that the *'de facto'* great winner countries of the cold war were China and Germany."

- "How about that?!"

- "According to Wikipedia, in 2017 the gross domestic product (GDP) of China was 12,250.39 billions of US dollars (USD); in 1977, it was 174.94 billions of USD (compared to US GDP of $2,086 billions in the same year). That means that in 40 years, between 1977 and 2017, the GDP increased 70 times. In an other article of Wikipedia, the China's gross domestic product based on purchasing power parity GDP (PPP) estimation, for 2018, was 25.1 trillions (Int'l$.). In 2017 the GDP of

US was 19,390.00 billions of USD and its estimation for the GDP (PPP) in 2018, was 20.2 trillions (Int'l$.). Now, the economies of US and China are the main economies of the world. Today China has the world's largest industrial output. As far as I know, those Chinese achievements have been possible due the way the cold war ended and due the historic trip of President Nixon to China. Without those events the launching of the recent Chinese lunar probe wouldn't have been possible either!"

- "I see what you mean, Dan. Probably you are absolutely right. I remember that from February 21 to 28, 1972, President Richard Nixon traveled to Beijing, Hangzhou, and Shanghai. This was the week that changed the world and eventually led to the collapse of the USSR and of the Communist Eastern bloc. In the morning of February 21, at 7 AM President Nixon left Guam and after 4 hours in the air, he arrived in Shanghai. From Shanghai, he travelled to Beijing. Almost as soon as the President Nixon arrived in the Chinese capital, Chairman Mao summoned him for a meeting. During his trip, President Nixon held also many meetings with Chinese Premier Zhou Enlai and other Chinese officials. I read that, from his first day in the White House, President Nixon began working to open a channel of communication with Beijing. To reach this end he had carried out a series of careful moves *t*hrough Communist *China's* allies *Romania and Pakistan*. In March 1972, a Gallup poll stated that more than fifty percent of the surveyed found President Nixon's trip to China effective in terms of improving world peace. But no one did actually surmise what will actually happen in the long run."

- "Amazing! Your interesting account made me remember a certain happening. You just said: *'to open a channel of communication with Beijing'*, President Nixon *'had carried out a series of careful moves through Communist China's allies Romania and Pakistan.'* By chance, I was involved in one of those *'moves'*. Starting on November 2, 1970 till the end of 1975, I was employed by the American multinational computer manufacturing corporation Control Data Corporation (CDC). At first I worked six months in its research and development department, then I was transferd to the CDC subsidiary for East Europe located in Vienna-Austria. My position was that of marketing manager for Romania, and later on, as market development, East Europe manager. In the summer of 1971, I received at my office in Vienna an urgent notice that I had the task of preparing a visit to Romania of an important delegation headed by Mr. Robert D. Schmidt, CDC Executive Vice President -the second person in the management of the firm. At the agreed date, I went to Bucharest to receive the delegation at the airport. The Executive Vice-President Schmidt and two other vice-presidents of CDC were dressed casually, the other three members of the delegation were in oficial evening costumes. They had some solemn faces, and they did not pronounce a word, no matter how much I tried to start various conversations with them. Apart from the fact that those guys did not seem to be from CDC, I was also surprised by the size of the delegation. Another surprise followed; they announced me that they did not want to negotiate with the Romanian authorities, but I had the task of arranging for them to be received at the Embassy of the People's Republic of China in Bucharest. Now that would seem a trivial matter, but that time -before President Nixon's visit to China- that was unimaginable. All the Chinese press was criticizing the *'American imperialists'* and the US was described as a *'paper tiger'*. China was on the so-called 'Z' embargo list, being considered the enemy of the United States. When I expressed my suprise, in the sense that I was expecting to be asked to arrange for the delegation to be received at the Romanian government or at any Romanian ministry, they told me to forget all that and solve the problem. During three days, we went to the Chinese embassy four times with the entire delegation, but each time we were treated with refusal. The Chinese at the entrance assured us that neither the ambassador nor the economic adviser were present in the embassy. When I told him that we wanted to be received by anyone, he replied that there was no one present in the embassy! On the second day after the arrival of the delegation, I came to the conclusion that, finally, the problem could only be solved in our usual Romanian style. My wife was member of the *'ladies group'* of the wife of an VIP in the Romanian government; to that group also belonged the wife of an Deputy Minister for Foreign Afaires etc. My wife asked all ladies in the group to demand their husbands to intervene at the Embassy of China, for the reception of the American delegation."

- "That time in Romania and in the other communist countries existed that kind of corruption, bribery and so on."

- "That's right Bill! Yet, the corruption in my country is considered nowadays to be even higher; at least, that is the feeling when you are listening to the opinions of the EU officials. But, let us come back to our subject. On the fourth morning, while we were taking breakfast at the Intercontinental

Hotel, the entire American delegation thought there was no point in insisting farther. Disappointed with the outcome of my démarches, I asked them to try again once more. We went again to the Embassy of China, where we were welcomed. In a large reception room, in semicircle there was an impressive number of Chinese people with solemn faces. During the reception we were served with tea. Although it was not sweetened, it was tasty with a special flavor. Only one of the Chinese spoke, in Chinese of course, another Chinese translated it into Romanian, and I was translating it into English. *'We have the pleasure,'* said the Chinese *'to welcome our American friends on Chinese territory, and to thank our very good Romanian friends for arranging this meeting.'* Compared to what I knew from the press about the *'Sino-American friendship'* of those times, I thought I did not hear well, so I asked him to repeat once more what he said. The Chinese told us again the same words. After the reception, the Americans praised my perseverance (in fact, my Transylvanian stubbornness). I could not master my curiosity and I asked one of the CDC vice-presidents, whether the guys in the black suits in the delegation (who did not say a word neither during the reception) were or not from the State Department. He answered me: *'No comment! You are not supposed to know!'* When President Nixon visited China, I was as amazed as many others. Even today, I wonder if the Embassy of China in Bucharest decided at the last minute to receive the American delegation as a result of the intervention of that *'ladies'* group, or the Chinese embassy simply waited for Beijing approval."

- "Quite exciting... Now, tell me why do you consider that Germany was also a *'de facto'* great winner country of the cold war?"

- "I already talked too much. That's not fair; you know much more than I do, so I am interested to listen to what you have to say about the subject.

- "OK! I consider that Germany was one of *'de facto'* great winners of the cold war, because after starting and losing two world wars, this country managed to come in the position to establish nowadays the rules of the game in the European Union. Also, because the Federal Republic of Germany swalowed, without war, the so called German Democratic Republic, a member country of the United Nations. I remember that during that reunion, I read in the newspapers that the British Prime Minister of that time was not that happy about the new *Greater Germany*; neither was happy the President of France. The British Prime Minister Margaret Thatcher told Gorbachev: *'We do not want a united Germany'*. In December 1989, she told European Union leaders at a Strasbourg summit: *'We defeated the Germans twice! And now they're back!'* On 20 January 1990, French President François Mitterrand told Thatcher that a unified Germany could *'make more ground than even Hitler had'* and that will remain only *'Romania and Bulgaria for the rest of us.'* Now we can see that he was over optimistic."

- "That's right! Nowadays, Germany's influence in those two countries is higher than of any other country in the world. But, go on!"

- " Italy's Giulio of Italy Andreotti joked *'I love Germany so much that I prefer to see two of them.'* Israeli Prime Minister Yitzhak Shamir publicly opposed Germany's unification, saying that *'a country that decided to kill millions of Jewish people will try to do it again.'* Strangely enough, it seems that the last President of the USSR, didn't care and did not give a damn that Germany was again reunited. At Gorbachev and Kohl's negotiations, in mid-July 1990, West Germany got the permission to incorporate East Germany, a country with a territory of 108,333 square kilometers and 16 million people; that country had previously been the most prosperous state in the Warsaw Pact. For granting that permission, it was decided that the dying USSR will be helped with German money. In fact, German Chancellor Kohl promised financial help aimed at stabilizing Soviet finances and agreed to pay the costs from withdrawing Soviet troops and resettling them in USSR. The total cost paid is unknown, but it was estimated at between $31 and $50 billion."

- "How did you find all those details?"

- "I read most of them on the net. About the German industry what can I say?! Germany does have today a first rate industry. I was told by one of my neighbors -who traveled all over Europe, last summer- that most of the luxury cars he saw during his trip were BMW and Mercedes cars. He did not see many Cadillac cars in Europe. In the GDP of Germany, its industry represents an important percentage. There is also a high percentage of industrial products in the German exports."

- "That's enough! You explained it much better than I would have been able to do it. By the way, recently I participated in a discussion of two intelligent and engaging Americans, with a few English speaking Romanians knowledgeable in world affairs. When I presented the same arguments regarding the fact that the *'de facto'* great winner of the cold war was China, the two Americans made no comments. One of the

Americans, a retired person from a career in International Business, just stated that nowadays industry represents only 10% of the GDP in USA. I can't believe that!"

- "Why not believe it? The quotes you gave from President Trump Inauguration Address show that actually the American industry represents now little in the GDP of USA."

- "I am sorry Bill, but it is hard to believe it, because in 1970, when I started my research and development work in USA, I could see that on the American territory existed the most formidable industry that produced the entire world commodity nomenclature. All the American products were most reliable. The productivity, efficiency and inventiveness of Americans were unrivaled in the whole world. How was it possible for a good size of the existing industry on the American territory to disappear?! Those are the reason for which I just can't believe it! By the way, I remember that during our first discussion, you said that before US entered in the second world war, in the American public opinion of that time, was heavily rooted the idea that the Americans no longer had to mingle in the mess of a new European war. It is precisely on this point that my question is based. Why, after the Second World War, the American public opinion did not oppose the same way an involvement in foreign wars?! Why did that famous *'American isolationism'* die?! After the defeat of Germany and Japan in World War II, the United States continued to participate substantially in wars that took place thousands of miles away from your country. US were involved in the wars in Korea, in Vietnam, in Yugoslavia, in Iraq, in Afghanistan and so on. Were those wars in the interest of the American people?"

- "Knowing the truth better than anybody else, President Donald Trump gave the answer to this question, saying: *'We wasted $6 trillion on wars in the Middle East, whereas we could have rebuilt our country twice, look at our bridges, airports, schools and hospitals , they are totally out-of-date...'* After the Second World War, the USSR intervened abroad only a few times and for a much shorter time. The interventions in Hungary (1956) and Czechoslovakia (1968) were military successes but political disasters for the Soviets. Their war in Afghanistan was a failure both in military and in political terms. These wars have also contributed to the collapse of the Soviet Union. Why the *'American isolationism'* died?! Because of the cold war! The *'containment'* of USSR was needed; i.e. the spread of communism had to be stopped. I understand all that! But, I don't know why we waged wars after the collapse of the Soviet Union and of the

Communist Block. Two wars in Iraq... I think that my feeling is in accordance with the opinion of President Trump, showed above."

- " OK, Bill. Regarding the actual winners of the cold war, I want to tell you that there is the following saying in Romanian: *'when two fight each other, a third party wins'* It is that true, or not?"

- "It is true sometimes."

- "I read that the cold war started in 1947 and ended in 1989-91. Was that the last one? What next, Bill? There will be other cold war in the near future?"

- "Could be. As for the starting year of the previous cold war, I have a different opinion. In the period of 1939-1941, the Soviet Union was happy to see the main West European countries exhaust their strength in a bloody war; trains loaded with oil and food were sent to Germany. *'De facto'*, that was a sort of cold war between Soviets and the western powers. After Hitler started his war against the USSR in June 1941, the western powers were happy to see the Soviets and Germany exhaust their strength in a war even bloodier. Only in June 1944, when the Red Army got quite close to Berlin, *the 'D Day'* started. Actually, between June 1941 and June 1944, the cold war of USSR continued with the western powers; that was in the same time with their bloody war against Germany. In our world, there are other sorts of wars that are going on as well; like hybrid wars, proxy wars, trade wars, cyber wars etc."

- "It is strange, in these days, they are waging cyber wars not only against states, governmental institutions or banks, but also against private citizens. I was hurt by a kind of cyber war too."

- "What do you mean?!"

- "Yes... I am not kidding. Approximately two years ago, when I started my computer - connected to the Internet- I was greatly amazed to read on the screen the following: *'Attention! Your files are encrypted. All of your files were protected by a strong encryption. What do I do? So, there are two ways you can choose: wait for a minute and get your price doubled!... or start obtaining the only solution... If you have really valuable data, you better not waste your time, because there is no other way...'* What I did? I did not pay the *doubled* price, as I didn't have that kind of money to be able to pay those robbers. In my files I had important quantities of data, including the text of the book titled **'Europe: to be, or not to be - that is the Question!'** Although the book was not successful, its text was valuable to me. Just the same, I was lucky enough, as I had the same text on a Memory Stick as well. So, I didn't give a damn that the crooks encrypted the text of the mentioned book located in the files of the computer. It seems that files are actually safe, only and only in computers that are not connected to the Internet. Now, I would like to hear your opinion about the trade war."

- "Since 2018, United States and China have been engaged in a trade war. Higher tariffs and other measures were applied by US and China. Actually, since 2012, the US trade deficit with China has increased. According to the United States Census Bureau, the deficit was US$ 315.1 billion in 2012 and US$ 375.7 billion in 2017. The 2017 trade deficit existed because imports from China were US$ 505.6 billion while U.S. exports to China were only US$ 129.9 billion. The deficit is estimated to rise to over US$ 410 billion in 2018. The biggest categories of China's imports from United States were commercial aircraft, soybeans, and cars. The US biggest imports from China were computers and accessories, cell phones, apparel, steel and footwear. The trade deficit is caused to the fact that the standard of living being much lower in China (i.e. lower wages to workers), the goods sell for the lowest prices. The other cause of the deficit is the exchange rate of US dollar to Chinese yuan. Due to the huge yearly deficit, China is the largest lender to the U.S. government (over US$ 1 trillion). That is over one quarter of US total public debt owned by foreign countries. The trade war consisted in imposing tariffs and quotas on the imports of Chinese steel, solar panels, washing machines and other goods. To stop theft of American intellectual property, the Trump administration asks China to remove requirements that to gain access to the Chinese market the American companies have to transfer technology to Chinese firms. China responded by imposing tariffs on the following imported goods from US: aluminum, airplanes, cars, pork, soybeans, fruit, nuts, and steel piping."

- "Your long and interesting exposition made me think that the American-Chinese trade war is, after all, a consequence of the fact that China was an actual winner of the cold war; otherwise, that country would not have been able to produce and to export such huge quantities of products and services."

- "I agree with you, Dan. By the way, from this discussion of ours, I could see that in the period of 1970-75 in which you were an employee of an American Multinational Corporation you got the impression that in the good old USA everything was good and beautiful; the tallest skyscrapers, the longest bridges, the most luxurious and spacious cars and the highest efficiency in the world."

- "Maybe the actual reason is the fact that when I traveled to foreign countries I was tempted to visit and notice only beautiful things and places. In America I traveled from Niagara Falls in the north, to Key West in the south; it is said that sometimes from there you could see Cuba. Then I traveled from New York, to the West to the Garden of Gods and across the Rocky Mountains. During the six months of work and two weeks of leave spent in US, I traveled over 40,000 miles by car. In the years that followed, alone or with my wife and/or my son, I traveled all over the US many times. The nature and the American landscapes are magnificent. A very good impression produced the splendid American forests. It could be seen that US authorities were taking appropriate measures to protect them; I think the same is true nowadays. This is unlike what happens in other countries where wild deforestation has catastrophic consequences for the world's climate. I can relate about significant cases of this kind, such as the deforestation of the Amazon rainforest, as well as the wild deforestation of forests in my country Romania and their export as logs. In these massive cuts of forests, especially from Transylvania, also participates a company from Austria; those

Austrians don't realize that even in their country, being situated nearby, eventually the negative consequences will appear - tornadoes, landslides etc. Most Romanians have a very good opinion about the Americans and their way of life. But they would not keep all that opinion if they knew with what fear my colleagues at Research and Development were expecting any moment to be laid off. During that time, government orders fell sharply; largely, the CDC computers production depended on them. At that time, President Nixon was about to agree with the Russians a reduction in strategic armaments (SALT 1). All my colleagues in research and development, and the factory workers also, were worried because, that time, it was very difficult to find another job. Nowadays is not easy to find a job either. Despite that, if the borders were completely opened, I think at least one billion foreigners would come to settle in the United States. America has been and has remained the main immigration country in the world. I read on the net that in a century, between 1820 and 1920, 34 million people immigrated to the United States. I have visited the Statue of Liberty several times. Every time, I was impressed reading the following quote from the sonnet of Emma Lazarus': *Give me your tired, your poor, your huddled masses yearning to breathe free."*

- "I see, Dan... Also, I have to tell you that America has been and still it is the main beneficiary of brain drain. A lot of bright people have emigrated to the United States; not just from poor countries but also from Western Europe. Albert Einstein, Teller, Tesla, Fermi, Von Braun, Sikorsky, Stravinsky, Nabokov, Toscanini and many others came to create in USA. Apart from the fact that you can always be laid off in the US, what else do you consider it made and makes life stressful? I want your frank opinion. Illustrate it please by concrete examples, not in general."

- "Okay, concrete examples. In the fall of 1970, for the first time, I went by the Metroliners high speed train from Philadelphia to New York. At the beginning I was delighted; thanks to its extraordinary speed and great comfort. As we approached New York, my delight disappeared because of the big garbage heaps around the railroad. It is true that garbage was stacked nicely, but it was still depressing. In May 1971 I made a trip with my wife to Chicago. When we approached Chicago, intending to swim, we stopped the car at the shores of Lake Michigan. Where the water had withdrawn, we could see hundreds and hundreds of dead fish on the sand. Others were with belly up on the surface of the water. We did not have the courage to swim in a lake where so many fish just died. Coming close to Downtown Chicago, one day without a cloud in the sky, we could not see any skyscrapers. Gradually, like they were blurred out by a cloud, they began to appear. In June 1971 I was with my wife at a riverbank rest area near the apartment we lived in -the river is called the Schuylkill River. While my wife was steaming the beef steak, I decided to get into the water and swim. I put a foot in the water, it had a pleasant temperature and it looked clean. I got into the water completely. To my surprise, close to shore, the river was not deep 0enough for swimming. I took a few steps toward the middle of the river, but I found out that the sand was filled with glass fragments and pieces of metal. I got quickly out of the water, leaving me with an unpleasant sensation at the feet. At that time -that is 48 years ago- the Transylvanian river near the village where I was born had crystal clear water up to three meters deep. As a teenager, during the summer vacations, I was swimming in that wonderful water. Today, the water of this river is polluted and smelling ugly, its maximum depth being 10 centimeters. The effects of the technological advance of nowadays reached that river as well."

- "Unfortunately, all over the world, the pollution of the planet has not been and is not taken seriously by the decision makers. I remember that in our previous discussions we also referred to the dangers of atomic energy and of the nuclear weapons. It's strange, but even a greater danger is constituted by the plastics and PET bottles; though when discovered, they seemed harmless. A million plastic bottles are bought around the world every minute and their number will jump up even higher in the future. In the oceans -in which is said life appeared initially on Terra- there are nowadays more plastics and PET bottles than fish. Believing that they are edible, ocean creatures eat plastics and PET bottles. If this phenomena is further amplified, it could lead to the death of the oceans and, ultimately, to the disappearance of human beings on earth. The human beings did hurt the environment on the planet Terra like no other creature. So, it is no wonder that some severe warnings were made. At the end of last century, Loren C. Eiseley said: *'If the human race is to survive into the next century, scientific technology will have to learn how to control the devastating forces it has unwittingly turned loose on the planet - the world's exploding population, the reckless pollution of the environment, the spiraling arms race and the expenditure of irreplaceable energy'*. Stephen William Hawking, an English theoretical physicist, cosmologist, in 2006 posed the following question on the Internet: *'In a world that is in chaos politically, socially and environmentally, how can the human race sustain another 100 years?'*. In May 5, 2017, he declared: *'In order to survive, the human species will need, no later than 100 years from now, to populate another planet.'* On statistical considerations, the American Professor Daniel Whitmire, who teaches mathematics at the University of Arkansas, has reached to a similar conclusion. He believes that life on our planet will be extinguished about 200 years after the industrial revolution and the invention of the radio, which took place 100 years ago. After that date, the environment will be so polluted that technological progress and life will no longer be possible."

- "As far as I know, the needed technology to solve the problems of pollution is available since many years ago. In 1973, I had to accompany a prospect customer to a factory where systems for the depollution of wastewater were produced. The factory, located in San Diego, was owned by the American Multinational Corporation whose employee I was that time. At the factory, an expert said in his interesting exposition the following: *'In the time gone by, the traditional approach was according to the saying that the solution to pollution is dilution; that is to say, the domestic or industrial wastewaters used to be discharged into rivers, into seas and oceans.*

Nowadays, the dilution is no longer a solution anymore; it does not solve the problem of pollution. Actually, we polluted all the running and standing waters; including the oceans. We need to do something different. We have the solutions. Sure, they cost money.' Everything he said is valid today, as well."

- "Certainly, solving the pollution means spending much money. That's the real problem, Dan. They spent *'$6 trillion on wars in the Middle East'*. Actually, nobody would have approved the spending of that huge amount of money, to solve the problem of wastewater discharged into rivers, seas and oceans! At a global level, today, around 80% of wastewater produced is discharged into the environment untreated, causing widespread water pollution. It is strange, but these days, the leaders of certain countries are promoting principally the sale of arms sales. No one promotes the sale of Levi's bluejeans; for sure, they can't promote the sale of that kind of products because they are not produced anymore in those countries."

- "By the way, I can tell you something regarding the subject dealt with. In the summer of 2018, I spent one week on the Greek seashore at Chalkidiki. From Bucharest to Thesaloniki I traveled by railway. When the train approached the Bulgarian border, being eager to see the *beautiful blue Danube* -as Johan Strauss Junior called it in his waltz- I opened the window of the railway car. When the train crossed the bridge, I was deeply disappointed; no *blue Danube* could be seen. The river's water was brown. I have to admit that close by, on the Romanian shore, uglier looking wastewater was being discharged in the Danube. Its dreadful smel was felt even in our railway car, so I had to close the window."

- "I guess that we talked enough about pollution. I would like to know what else you, as an alien i.e. European, feel that life is somehow peculiar in US."

- "That's a strange question indeed! OK, I will try to answer your question. I can see that you are a cultivated and cultured person and read more than I did. You do know much more than I do. Another cultured American friend of mine, Ted Ricci is his name and worked in the same company with me, used to go in the desert or on a mountain peak to listen symphonic music. From two stereo loudspeakers placed on the car, he was listening to symphonies by Beethoven, Tchaikovsky, Mozart... He told me that symphonic music sounds great in the desert or on a mountain peak. In spite of two examples, I got the impression that most Americans either don't love culture enough, or that to them culture means something else than what it means to us Europeans. I hope that I will be capable show you what I mean. In the automatic laundry of the apartment house where I lived near Philadelphia, waiting for my laundry to be washed and dried, I had long discussions with a lady teacher, who was teaching English literature at a high school. She was surprised that, just with technical schooling, I had read more than she did of the works of the great American writers Cooper, Melville, Mark Twain, Jack London, Dreiser, Fitzgerald, Dos Passos, Hemingway, Faulkner, Steinbeck, Mailer, Salinger, Nabokov, Bellow, Hailey, Sinclair Lewis, Arthur Miller, Tennessee Williams and Michener. Though I was working and living most of the time among Americans with university studies, I found out that most of those I met had not been, all their life, at a theater performance, nor at a symphonic concert or an opera show."

- "I do appreciate your frank answer. Now, let see how we stand with the inequality in this world of ours. According to TV shows, newspapers, magazines and meetings in Davos, the inequality in the world has increased continuously. It was said that in 2018, the 26 richest persons on the Terra had the same net worth as some 3.8 billion people that are the poorest half of the world's population. *'It is obscene for so much wealth to be held in the hands of so few when 1 in 10* *people survive on less than $2 a day. Inequality is trapping hundreds of millions in poverty; it is fracturing our societies and undermining democracy.'* That was the adequate declaration made, in January 2017, by the Executive Director of Oxfam International. In the year of 2015 the GDP per capita in the country with the richest population of the world (Luxemburg) was 366 times higher than the GDP per capita in the poorest country (Burundi)! After three years, i.e. in 2018, Luxembourg's GDP per capita has increased to 113,954 USD and was 371 times higher than GDP per capita of South Sudan which was US $307. Of 194 countries, only 16 countries have per capita income above $50,000. If the current world status quo remains unchanged, the existing few rich countries will become even richer in the future, while the numerous poor countries will become even poorer. It is a bigger inequality inside all countries, whether they are rich or poor. Inequality between rich and poor people will continue to grow faster and faster!"

- "I attended an academic seminar, in which it was said, that due the real material possibilities of the planet Terra and of the accelerated environmental pollution, the current American consumer society would be possible only for a total of one billion inhabitants; the one existing in West

Europe for maximum 3 billion. But, now over 7 billion people live on our planet; compared to 1.6 billion at the beginning of the twentieth century! In this world of ours, a few nations and a few people can be very rich and can have a very high standard of living, only and only if there are many poor countries and many poor people."

- "I don't know, Dan... Maybe, those assertions are correct ones. I have to admit also that even in my country there are a lot of Americans who are just debtors to the banks - credit card debt, student loans, mortgages and the like- and have negative wealth. Wait a minute, I will look on the net to see the percentage of those unfortunate..."

- "You don't have to waste time to look for any percentage... The Americans are hard working, maybe the hardest working people in whole world. So, logically it is not acceptable any percentage you could find. Unacceptable is also the fact that those unfortunate have to pay for their credit cards debts, outrageous interest rates! The millionaires have to pay low interests for their loans, while the poor pay much, much higher interest rates; that is completely immoral!"

- "I see that you are a real idealist and I sympathize with you, my friend. But no banker would do the same. All bankers in the world are concerned with one thing only and that is to get back, as fast as possible, all money his bank lent the poor; plus the highest interest that can be applied. *'Money is power; hence, corporate greed; it's never enough.'* To that sensible appreciation, made by your former daughter in law Susan, I would add banks greed."

- "You are right Bill! I know a specific case in which somebody has to pay for his huge credit cards debts over 20% -even 23%- interests per year! At those huge interest rates, he already actually paid his debts; nevertheless, he is still indebted to the banks and will continue to pay in the future. That person being over indebted, he got a very harsh treatment from the banks; in other way around, those who are in good financial standing get a lenient treatment. By the way, I do know that those greedy bankers and millionaires will not take with them their money to the Heavens. For their greed, I suppose that they will be sent straight to the deepest corner of Hell."

- "I hope you are right. It is much talking about migrants, not just in Europe but in US, as well. So, I would like to hear your opinion on this topic."

- "One of the friends of mine sent me an email regarding the migrants in Europe. The email says that a study, from 2018, by the World Health Organization reveals that in some European countries the number of migrants is 3-4 times higher than that is pointed out by official documents. In that study is said that the total number of the migrants in Europe is actually around 91 million persons; that is 10% of Europe's current population. By country, the number of migrants and the respective percentage of the country's population are: Germany - 12.1 million (14.8%), England - 8.8 million (13.4%), France - 7.9 million (12.2%), Italy - 5.9 million (10%), Spain - 5.9 million (12.8%), Turkey - 4.8 million (6.1%), Switzerland - 2.5 million (29.6%), the Netherlands - 2 million (12.1%), Sweden - 1.7 million (17.6%), Austria - 1.6 million (18.2%), Belgium - 1.2 million (11%), Greece - 1.2 million (11%), Hungary - 0.5 million (5.2%) and Romania - 0.37 million (1.9%). I assume that those are correct figures. Those who don't believe the respective numbers, have to look on the TV to see any football matches of the French national team; some of those who compose it no longer resemble the characters in Alexandre Dumas, Dumas Fils, Balzac, or Hugo novels -i.e. D'Artagnan, Athos, Porthos, Aramis, Gavroche and so on; now they are a mix of genuine Frenchmen with Africans, Asians, Arabs etc. Looking at the matches of the national football teams of England, and Belgium, for example, they could see the same reality. In a recent TV show, was said that the percentage of genuine British persons accounts for less than 50% of London's population. The Mayor of London is a Pakistani. In the future, fundamental changes could happen to the population structure of Great Britain, France, Germany and of the other rich West European countries. Especially, in those countries the percentage of the non-whites will probably rise very much in the next 30 to 40 years. By the way, I would like to point out that the current migration of the most competitive part of the East European labor force to West Europe is particularly advantageous for rich Western countries. For the former so called 'Eastern socialist countries', the consequences are catastrophic. After spending their tiny financial funds for schooling, the best-prepared East Europeans settle in rich countries to enrich the rich. For the reasons showed in our first discussion -the great inequality between rich and poor countries and due to the local wars- the number of migrants that will arrive in western countries will increase continuously."

- "The Americans are concerned more about the migrants coming to settle themselves in US. You said that *'if the borders were completely opened, at least one billion foreigners would come to settle in the United States.'* I am sure that you know in detail what is discussed in my country about the wall with Mexico."

- "In 1973, I spent eight days in Mexico. That time, the population of Mexico was 54.30 million people."

- "Yeah... Since that time the population of Mexico has increased very much, Dan. In 2018, it reached 130.76 million people. If a lot of Mexicans had not migrated to US, the population of Mexico would have been even higher. I read in one of the Robert D. Kaplan books that most of those Mexican immigrants live in Texas, New Mexico, Arizona, California, Nevada and Utah. Also, I read in the same book that part of those States had been in Mexico, before the war for the Independence of Texas (1835-36) and the Mexican-American war of 1946-48. According to Robert Kaplan, not many Mexicans go to Florida; the Florida State is preferred by the former citizens of Cuba. Both Mexicans and Cubans, and all the other nations of the Latino-American countries as well, have a lot of children. It seems, that less schooled the nations are and lower standard of living they have, more children they have."

- "That applies to myself and my two brothers, as well. My brother that was an electrician with seven years of elementary school - he graduated three of those years, after he got married- has three daughters and one son. My youngest brother graduated high school and has two daughters and one son. Myself I am university graduate and I have only 1 son. The children of my brothers are married and have well-to-do families, but each of them have only one child. My son has no children. So, the rule mentioned by you applies to the new generation also."

- "I see that it applies to Romanians too… It is strange that even well off Mexicans are eager to migrate to United States. A young friend of mine intended to marry a girl that was the actual human resources manager at Lufthansa Global Business Services in Mexico. That is an important position, as she was responsible for hiring new employees and supervising employees' evaluations at a Lufthansa Company located in a country that was in the past and still is today very important for Germany. After some time, that friend of mine got the feeling that she didn't love him at all; she was just interested to get out of Mexico and to acquire a green card to work and live in US. In books, magazines, newspapers and accessing Google, I read a lot about the structure of US population; the present and the future one. For example, I read that there are more than one million Hispanic residents in ten US states, respectively in Texas, Florida, New Mexico, Arizona, California,

Colorado, Georgia, Illinois, New Jersey and New York. Or that today, only Mexico has a larger Hispanic population than US. Not just Mexicans are eager to come and settle in US, but also the other Hispanic people from South and Central America. It was estimated that, by 2060, non-whites will rise and will make up 57 percent of the US population; 28.6% of that, with 119 million, will be Hispanic individuals. By 2060, the non-Hispanic whites will be only 43% of the overall US population (currently 62%). The percentage of Asians will rise from 6% to 14% and the Afro-Americans will be 13% (12% now). No ethnic group will have majority. So, the structure of US population by 2060 will be similar with the structure existing at the present time in Latino-American countries. I don't know if, by 2060, all that was estimated will really hapen."

- "Nobody knows, I guess."

- "I would like to add that all those important topics, are too vast. For example, one of those is the subject of globalization. Everything we discussed has, somehow, connection with the nowadays globalization. I think that it is significant just to reveal the following swift increases: in cross-border movement of capital, goods, services and technology, in movement of people -including migrants, tourists and students-, in soil, air and water pollution and in income inequality. You said that half of Romania's emploees moved to rich countries. The main reason for that is the fact that in the European Union people can move freely between member states to live, study, work and retire in another country. Certainly, the Romanians moved also to other countries, including US; as your son did.

- "From June 20 to August 30, 2008, together with my wife, I was in US. During that time the United States was in a severe financial crisis combined with a deep recession, which lasted from December 2007 to June 2009. I am sure that you remember that there was a slow recovery; it took several years for the economy to recover to pre-crisis levels of output and employment. As my son Daniel just moved in a new rented house situated close to one of the *Finger Lakes* in New York States, we decided to invite some of his friends to a Danube Delta Romanian style dinner. As all the guests were cultivated and some who got a prosperous situation by their own forces, the discussions turned to the financial crisis. One of them was the owner of two small companies of manufacturing and research and development in optical field, another one was a successful medical doctor who owned several buildings that were rented, a young lady was in real estate business and the last one was a highly qualified expert in computers. Mainly, all of them blamed the globalization -economic, political, cultural, ecological and even ideological- for their serious problems. They were complaining that due the globalization, steadily, not just the manufacturing of most consumer products was transferred abroad, but some of the specialized goods and equipment as well. For example, the owner of the optical companies said that he had to lay off some of his employees, due to the fact that Chinese companies were delivering certain optical components at much lower prices than those that can be realized in US. Also it was said that for the first time in the post-war period, in US the average living standard of the previous generation was higher than that of the current generation. At that time, I mean the summer of 2008, I was surprised to hear all that, so I told them: *'the perception of most Europeans that I know of is that the nowadays globalization means westernization, or rather, Americanization. It was initiated and promoted by the United States. It's your work! It resulted from Pax-Americana, from America's dominant economic, political and military position. Globalization has expanded even further after the US remained the only superpower in the world. It is strange that now, you are complaining about it yourselves!'* Just the same, all our guests continued to be opposed to the globalization."

- "Most of US citizens with high school and college education became more and more opposed to the globalization. I read on the Internet that in an 1997 poll, 58% of the American college graduate respondents said globalization was good; by 2008 the percentage fell to 33%. The residents of Asia and Africa tend to view globalization more favorably than those of North America and Europe. Our first discussion, Dan, was in the summer of 1999; at that time, a good part of the American industry was already transferred abroad. Later on, as far as I know, its transfer became even faster. So that in January 20, 2017, truthfully was said: *'One by one, the factories shuttered and left our shores, with not even a thought about the millions upon millions of American workers left behind.'* An intermediate stage existed in 2008, when you discussed the globalization subject with the guests at the Romanian style dinner. We know the unfolding. Sincerely, I do not know when and how the American industry will actually return to the *'landscape of our nation'*. I do hope that it will return eventually. Right now, I remembered that we didn't refer to the fact that the pollution of our planet is caused also by nowadays' agriculture; we eat too much meat and too many products obtained by genetic mutation, pesticides and chemicals are used in excess etc. We didn't say a single word about the fact that pollution is also due to the fact that everybody - companies, banks, most people- are just interested to make money. Providing that you make money, almost nobody really cares much about pollution. Living in free countries, we presented with sincerity our opinions on the above mentioned controversial topics. We do know that many others will not agree with our opinions. That is all right and we would be happy to discuss the differences of opinion; in case that it will be demonstrated that we are wrong we will change our mind. Telling all that, I suggest our discussions should be finished now. Do you agree?"

- "That's OK with me, Bill. Good luck and thank you."

- " Good-bye! Thank you too."

August 15, 2019

www.ingramcontent.com/pod-product-compliance
Lightning Source LLC
Chambersburg PA
CBHW070458220526
45466CB00004B/1874